CHRISTIAN MARRIAGE

CHRISTIAN MARRIAGE

Sacrament of
Abiding Friendship

JOHN & THERESE BOUCHER

Resurrection Press
Mineola • New York

To Our Children
Rachel, Peter, Mary, Tim and Katie
who have taught us so much about love

Published in 1995 by Resurrection Press, Ltd.
P.O. Box 248
Williston Park, NY 11596

Second printing – November 1995

Copyright © 1995 by John and Therese Boucher

ISBN 1–878718–25–8

Cover design by John Murello

Printed in the United States of America.

Contents

Foreword

HOW WONDERFUL to see a book on marriage whose approach is positive and uplifting! The Bouchers have a gentle and loving touch with one another that clearly comes out in their writing. They treat the love relationship of a man and woman in the Sacrament of Matrimony as a wonderful opportunity to develop mutual potential for growth in the capacity to love.

It is so good to see marriage approached in a non-clinical way. It often seems that marriage is treated by those who write about it as a sociological or psychological happening (sometimes even an ordeal). Therese and John come to us with the perspective of sharing a lived experience. The aura of reality pervades this small book. It is evident throughout, that the suggestions they make and the advice they give are the result of how they have worked and loved together. What a breath of fresh air!

What most comes to mind in reading their joint effort is how down to earth and real they are. This is a sharing not a preaching. They describe marriage as something normal and within the reach of all of us. There is no sense that we have to make enormous sacrifices. They constantly offer hope and reassurance. Also, there is no taking sides or gender politics. They are both on the same side, the side of love.

The whole book is most helpful but two chapters especially stand out, they are on Recreation and Hard Times. Their gentle practicality was most effective in those situations.

It was a delight to experience the faith that permeates their relationship. They are real believers. While not ideological in any way, they obviously have a deep trust in God and allow the divine to be a source of strength and direction in their continuing growth in mutual love and affection. They are completely natural and unembarrassed in their faith.

The book is easy reading, very gentle and persuasive. All couples will profit from sharing in the Bouchers' love experience.

CHARLES A. GALLAGHER, S.J.
January 8, 1995

~ 1 ~

Sacrament of Abiding Intimacy

HAVE YOU EVER had one of those long days when even the driveway looks endless? Have you ever climbed out of the car imagining an enthusiastic greeting from your spouse, a table set with your favorite meal, and a whole evening of uninterrupted relaxation together? A popular video store has a television ad about such an evening. The climax of the ad occurs when the husband hides a ringing telephone in a desk drawer.

Husbands and wives need time together, as well as the opportunity to explore their hopes and dreams. Married couples need an attentive kind of mutual support that re-creates, and sustains; unless both are willing to settle for an impersonal level of cohabitation. Couples need an active intimacy that involves sharing time, thoughts, feelings, and activities.

One of the greatest hopes in marriage is that the relationship itself can be an abiding source of friendship, re-creation and support. The dictionary definition of "abide" gives clues to the characteristics of such a friendship: "to wait for, to accept, to endure with, to trust, and to remain stable." Husbands and wives can experience all this through the abiding friendship of Christian marriage.

One of the most crippling diseases in our world is the absence of an unfolding friendship between spouses. We need mutual acceptance and stability in order to face each other's needs and expectations, as well as the needs of the relationship itself. We need an abiding intimacy, grounded in God's love, that filters into all areas of shared life: communication, sexuality, spirituality, recreation, and work. Then each of these avenues for intimacy can become a new environment for growth.

This chapter will consider spiritual intimacy — our mutual struggle to understand deeply human experiences, the common quest for the meaning of life, and the ability to share faith in our God. Chapters two and five will cover relational intimacy — ways we pay attention to building a marriage, such as conversation and resolving conflict. Chapter three will cover the ways we balance all these kinds of intimacies for a richer marriage. Suggestions for greater sexual intimacy will be considered in Chapter four. Finally, Chapter six will consider the outgoing nature of an abiding friendship.

God's Abiding Presence

This kind of friendship doesn't just happen, but takes time and effort on a daily basis. Couples need ways to back off from demanding work situations and enjoy each other. We take long walks to the sod farm at the end of our street, in order to give an ear to each other's needs. Therese finds it easier to share while walking, especially when she is discouraged. John needs the exercise to maintain good health and enjoys combining this personal need with the needs of our relationship.

The good news is that God is beside us as we travel many roads together, as we greet one another, and even as we fail to be there for one another. God's abiding presence is at the root and foundation of the sacrament of marriage. Eternal and unshakeable Life is always available to us, like the clear refreshing waters of an artesian well supplying our homes. God wants to nurture, heal, sustain and even challenge us to grow together. God can magnify the good between us, giving comfort and erasing the pain.

The Old Testament story of Tobiah and Sarah in the Book of Tobit (Ch 5–10) has been an inspiration for us. They married in the midst of many problems, but they were confident in God and the holiness of their love for one another. The Scripture tells us that the first thing they did as a married couple was to pray aloud together (Tob 8:4–9). In doing so, Sarah was freed from evil and Tobiah was strengthened. Their joy in God's goodness became the basis for their relationship.

We aren't always interested in praying together like Sarah and Tobiah, or even aware of God's presence. Some years ago, Therese was overwhelmed by the care of two preschoolers and a difficult pregnancy. John encouraged her to pray, but was met with angry glares. Therese recalls:

"After a litany of my complaints at the supper table, John asked if I had talked to God about my feelings. I stormed out of the room and slammed the bathroom door behind me. God heard about the diapers, the broken flower pot, the nausea, the exhaustion. I just need a few minutes of relaxation, not prayer, I complained. 'I just need time to forget and have fun. You're no fun God!'

"Then I stopped and took a long slow breath. It was time to listen and give God a chance to answer back. What I heard was a voice echoing in my heart. 'Well, Therese, right now you aren't much fun either!' "

Mixing Belief and Marriage

Every marriage is a mixed marriage when it comes to faith. Each of us fades in and out of realizing God's loving presence. Each of us has a unique spirituality. What we have in common is a desire to find meaning in life, even when on vacation from belief, even when God is only a silent partner in life. Jesus has answered this common desire. Jesus has made promises to us as married couples.

It is up to us to seek his refreshment, healing, and forgiveness. His answers are beyond our wildest dreams, beyond the idea of living "happily ever after," more glorious than an unending honeymoon. Second, fifth, and thirteenth honeymoons are always possible because of God's unlimited love for us as couples.

Perhaps the gift that Jesus offers is like the rose-colored blanket that we received as a wedding gift. We still don't know who gave it to us. There was no card, no relative upset by not receiving a thank you. The love of

Father, Son and Spirit has been given to strengthen and warm us, even though it may seem to be anonymous. But imagine how much more can happen, as such a gift is acknowledged. Imagine discovering new levels of friendship rooted in a source beyond and yet beside us.

A Closer Look at the Sacrament

This sacrament of abiding friendship empowers us to support each other, to affirm, to forgive, to do so many things that make us one. In daily life the depths and nature of this oneness are put to the test. The challenge of spiritual intimacy lies in how we answer the question, "Which *one* do we become?" It is not a question of which personality wins. The strength of our sacramental union is that we are called to become the *one* body of Jesus, to be bound by an invisible but unbreakable thread. "We have come to know and to believe in the love God has for us. God is love, and whoever [abides] in love [abides] in God and God in him" (1 Jn 4:16).

Look at the Kind of Friendship You Have Together

Pope John Paul II in his 1981 "Apostolic Exhortation on the Family" says that the first task of a family is to "become more and more what it is, a community of life and love." How are you building a common life together? What does each of you expect of the other and of your marriage? Personal feelings and expectations can fuel a healthy relationship or erupt like a mass of molten lava. They can be very knowable and clear, or difficult to express. Building a healthy marriage requires the hard work of respecting another's emotions and ideas, even when they seem foreign.

Look at How You Both Feel about God

When life gets crazy, we can feel that God is very distant. In a sense, each of us expects either too little or too much from God. Even then God is big enough to listen to our feelings and needs. The reality is that God has chosen and "espoused" each of us, giving us the strength to espouse one another. Do you want an intimate relationship with God? Do you expect to see God in your daily life?

Does God have a place in your marriage, in your home, even in your sexual encounters? How do you live out the option of spiritual intimacy in your marriage? How do you air your feelings about God? A new car or a leisurely meal together in a restaurant can be a time to thank God. St. Paul's prayer for families comes to mind. "May Christ dwell in your hearts through faith; that you, rooted and grounded in love, may have strength to comprehend... the breadth and length and height and depth...the love of Christ" (Eph 3:17–19).

Look at What You Believe about God

Do you believe that God loves you and that God loves your spouse? Have you experienced the presence of Father, Son and Holy Spirit? What personal beliefs or creeds do you have? The creeds we recite in church are meant to be bare skeletons of a vital relationship with God, lived out in the midst of God's people. Creeds can also outline our struggles with areas of belief and disbelief in everyday life. You might compare the statements in a creed that you hold firm and others that are a struggle.

Look at God's Presence in your Marriage

Your friendship has sacramental dimensions in good times and even in times that batter the human heart. Look for the high points. These are times of blessing from God. Look for the low points. Wasn't there a small voice whispering an invitation to change, repentance and healing? God cares about each year and each day of your marriage. God is a part of the concerns of daily life, a part of the crises, and part of any fresh new intimacy in your shared life. God is even present when we can't love a spouse, when we feel like giving up on each other. Jesus came to touch the broken and the empty, to destroy walls of hostility. "For he is our peace, he who made both one and broke down the dividing wall...that he might create in himself one new person in place of two" (Eph 2:14–15).

Celebrating God Together

A period of great joy in your marriage can be like a second honeymoon in God's sight. Large and simple pleasures are gift. Gratitude to God brings hope about new blessings in your marriage. Our joy at our son Tim's birth led us to thank God aloud for him in the delivery room, despite the presence of an unknown, masked obstetrician. The intensity of the event was enriched by thanking God.

A few days after Tim's birth, John was still filled with enthusiasm and joy. While he was teaching a session for parents of first Communion children, a man stood up to ask a question about family prayer. John told our story about praying together in the delivery room as part of his answer to the man's question. The more details John provided the more quizzical the man became. John finished by saying, "We knew just how amazing God's love is. Does that answer your question?"

"Why yes," Dr. Faricy replied with a grin. "I know what you mean. I was there. I was the doctor!"

It is also very important to rejoice and to acknowledge the goodness of God reflected in a spouse. Anniversaries and birthdays can be times to tell one another the specific attributes we enjoy. Aren't there things we can say that are just as meaningful as the words we buy from Hallmark? We can also take the time to thank God in prayer, both privately or together. Whatever makes you happy can be a gateway to rejoicing in God and renewing your commitment to each other.

Our world is disillusioned about the abiding nature of marriage itself. Our world is bereft of a source of healing when marriages falter. Choosing marriage as an abiding spiritual friendship puts us on a firm foundation. God has pitched a tent among us. Jesus has set the table in our homes. The Holy Spirit pours out refreshing streams of eternal life. You can be held and upheld together by God. Talk to Jesus. Expect great things to happen as you join God in the kitchen, in the bedroom, in the car, and in the deepest recesses of your relationship.

Suggestions for Sharing and Prayer

1. Make a list of things you like about your spouse. Share your lists with one another. Thank God for your spouse by praying a "Glory Be" aloud together or take turns thanking God aloud for each of the items on your lists.

2. How do you feel about the kind of marriage you have? How is your spouse a friend? Each person can write a response. Then letters can be exchanged and acknowledged.

3. "it's not two ones are two
    but two are halves of one"
                                    e e cummings

What is your response to this poem? How could it be a description of your marriage?

4. How have you experienced God's presence or absence in your life and in your marriage? What do you want or expect from God?

~ 2 ~

Nurturing the Husband-Wife Relationship

WE ENJOY asking married couples how they met, or what their marriage proposal was like. Both people come to life as they remember early moments of joy and passion. We'd like to share two events from our own story just to jog your memory.

John recalls, "Therese waded into a sea of admirers that night at Hogan campus center. She was a leader in the small Christian community I had just joined. Though a serious bout with bronchitis had reduced her to a wisp of a woman, it seemed as though everyone wanted to hug her, talk to her, or hear some important word. Next to her I felt like an outcast or a spiritual pygmy. She stirred up deep passions within! At first I hated her guts."

Therese remembers a much later episode. "We were walking along Water Street next to the canoe factory after a day's work in a parish neighborhood center. John was unusually quiet. Then he came to an abrupt stop that brought us face to face. He took a deep breath and asked, "Therese will you marry me?" I responded with a "Yes." We resumed our walk, then half a block later he asked again. The following week at the beach he asked me several more times. Each time I heard more love and joy in his voice and less disbelief at my answer."

Think about what it was like for you when you met each other. Do you remember how your spouse became a source of wonder and discovery? What impressed you? Remember your declaration of love for each other, and how each of you became a central character in the other's life story. Remember how this drama propelled you toward a life-long choice of ongoing passion, like so many centuries of lovers.

One of the challenges of marriage is to maintain an interest in the events and the personal story of a spouse. Another is to see husband or wife as a main character, a kind of hero or heroine, rather than a villain or vixen. As we bring our stories together, God actually writes a new salvation story that involves both partners. What is your story and history as a married couple? If you had to pick out a theme song what would it be? Ours would be "Unchained Melody" by the Righteous Brothers. It celebrates a couple's desire for each other and adds the prayer, "God speed your love to me."

Balancing Revelation and Listening

Sharing life's unfolding story is a two-sided experience, something we try to practice at supper time. Each one of us shares the events of the day, and how these events touched and shaped us. The other person offers the gift of listening. Which role is more comfortable for you, or for your spouse? Do you switch roles often? One of the avenues for maintaining the intimacy of a relationship is this two-sided gift of revelation and acceptance.

The skill of active listening is an important ingredient in marriage. This means following what a spouse is saying, without clinging to a private agenda of words. It also means that after the other is finished, we can repeat the gist of the story, and especially the feelings behind it to our spouse's satisfaction.

An example of the distance that can come between us when we don't listen is a cartoon by Glasbergen that portrays a puzzled gentleman on his office phone. It reads "Hi, this is your wife. To find out what's for dinner, press 1. To apologize for something you said, press 2. To say 'I love you,' press 3. . . . "

Instead, active listening involves a letting go of needs, a confidence that needs will be met, a belief that perfect love is underneath us, like the solid earth after a plane trip. Too often, it is easy to think that a spouse should know, understand, and anticipate needs. When this happens, we must realize that neither husband nor wife is God, but together we can rely on God's Spirit to give gifts of peace, patience, perseverance, and understanding.

We must also appreciate the silence that punctuates our lives and represents the space between us, the vital need for solitude and independence. Sometimes there are no feelings or thoughts when we stop to look inside. Can we be at peace with a remark like, "I would rather not talk about it right now?"

As we enter into each other's world, a new compassion is possible. St. Paul's Letter to the Ephesians invites us to "preserve the unity of the Spirit through the bond of peace: one body and one Spirit, as you were also called to the one hope" (Eph 4:3–4). God's Spirit is offered to us as we work to create a harmony of mind and emotion, not a sameness, but a oneness. It takes humility, trust and perseverance to place the deeply held need to be understood at the feet of a loved one.

Jack discovered how isolated his deaf wife felt after he had a double ear infection. Before his experience he had often been impatient with her need for repetition. Now, he stops and holds her hand when she doesn't understand him.

Martha used to get angry at Phil because he wasn't able to relate to her and the children at the supper table. By listening more closely, she learned that he needed a half hour alone to unwind after a demanding day at work, and heavy traffic on the way home. Delaying supper was a helpful solution.

Affirmation Fosters Wholeness

Another part of Paul's Letter to the Ephesians talks about one of the goals of family and marriage. Through God, may you "be strengthened with power through his Spirit in the inner self, and that Christ may dwell in your hearts" (Eph 3:16–17). Paul points toward the idea that we can nurture one another's inner life. We can affirm the goodness that we experience in a spouse, which is an inner core or flame of God's goodness. We can give each other new strength through affirmation.

Therese is willing to see the adventure in little things like getting caught in the rain or a toddler's fascination with kitchen cabinets. John's firm grip on reality saves a lot of grief when estimating how long a trip will take, or when a college student will need to visit home. What small and large gifts do you see in your spouse? What acts of kindness or compassion shine through routine activities performed for the benefit of others? It's good to compliment a spouse, to be a mirror.

It's easy to remember the first time Therese complimented John in front of his mother. He had just read a story to the children. "John, you really brought those characters to life. That was great. Thanks." Mom was flabbergasted. She teased us by patting herself on the back and exclaimed, "Boy am I wonderful!" Giving and receiving affirmation was something foreign to Mom. For us too, it was a new skill to cultivate in the early years of our marriage, and one we still work at now. We hope that affirming one another is more common in our marriage than critical remarks or backhanded humor; but you would have to ask our children how we are doing.

Communicating Despite Limits

We need to grow in "relational intimacy," and give attention to our marriage, even communicating about our limitations. One author talks about our unresolved differences as "furniture" that we bump into in the dark. For us, an example would be heated remarks about different driving styles. Each of us brings frustrations, attitudes, limitations, and even sin into our marriages. So it is normal for conflicts to arise.

The patterns you have for handling conflicts are an important part of the communication between you. How does each spouse react to episodes of broken communication? How do you re-establish your relationship after an impasse? Are you both able to say, "I'm sorry" when real damage has been done? What kind of ground rules are there for disagreements and unresolved issues? We would propose some guidelines based on the good news of God's forgiveness.

1. Begin with "I statements" about needs, feelings and events. Avoid making accusations and drawing conclusions about your partner in the early part of a conversation. An example would be, "I feel rejected when you come home late."

2. State what you saw the other person do and how you felt in response. We hope to confront actions without attacking personal identity or worth. "Wet dirty clothes on the bedroom floor make me feel nauseous. Can you help me with this?"

3. Respect your spouse's emotions, without trying to solve the other's inner conflict. Let each spouse be responsible for personal feelings. One wife was relieved to realize that she didn't have to calm her husband down whenever

the neighborhood kids cut through their yard. A better starting point for her was, "This really gets you angry. What would you like to do about these kids?"

4. Try to look at a difficult situation together. Take turns stating your point of view. Take a few minutes to change places in an argument by writing down what you hear your partner saying. It may be helpful to consider God's point of view also. Did anything like this ever happen to Jesus? How did he act?

5. Concentrate on the present situation. Try reporting any cartoon-like fantasies connected with difficult feelings. For example, "I'm mad enough to spit poison!" or "I'm scared enough to crawl into a cave and set a guard dog at the entrance." Try to leave the past alone, instead of seeing life as one overwhelming complaint.

6. Get help if there are certain conflicts that recur often, especially if you feel like you are re-reading an old script from a dangerous nightmare. There are people who can help you as individuals and as a couple.

John went through a year of therapy when we were first married. Before each session we would pray together. During that year he was able to sort out difficult feelings and experiences associated with being a father. John's therapist was amazed at the amount of progress he made.

Communication is the Basis for Decision Making

The way you communicate affects every other area of your life together. It's important to realize that each couple's patterns of communication are the foundation for decision-making abilities. Decisions about finances, time, sexuality, career needs, and family are made in whatever atmosphere you have established for talking to each other. If you are able to share thoughts, feelings, perceptions, and information in day-to-day sharing, then more fruitful discussions about important decisions are possible.

It could be said that making decisions is a specialized kind of communication, an event that nurtures or strains your relationship. How are family decisions made? Who decides what? Who has the last word? Do you have a successful way to decide important things together?

One approach to making decisions involves the following steps:

1. Determine the question or questions involved. Three years ago we considered moving to a nearby town. Questions were: Should we move? Should we move now? Should we move to the Lambert's apartment in Melville?

2. Write down the pros and cons for the question you have chosen to answer first. List the facts, feelings, and issues involved on both sides of the question. Everything listed is important. Consider personal needs, your relationships, and responsibilities involved.

3. Discuss a few possible actions together, until both people can feel, think and imagine what these alternatives would be like. Then decide.

We did move to Melville and learned a lot about each other's needs for stability and living space during the decision-making process. It was even helpful to reminisce about previous moving experiences before we decided.

Suggestions for Sharing and Prayer

1. Write a description of your first meeting, and then of your marriage proposal. Compare stories. What do these events say about your relationship then and now?

2. Choose a fairy tale, movie or song that reminds you of your marriage. What does it say about your relationship? What are your dreams for the future?

3. Tell each other one good thing you've seen your spouse do lately. How do you want to be understood? In what ways do you need to be listened to and appreciated?

4. How do you feel about the patterns you have for disagreeing? Are your conflicts more like: a wrestling match, a duel with pistols, being stranded in a blizzard, or fighting a nuclear war? Why? (Share "I" statements only.)

5. Write a forgiveness prayer together, using concrete examples of your own failures. For example: "When I storm out of a room and refuse to listen, Lord have mercy." Begin praying this litany together with a reading of Ephesians 2:13–18. End with an "Our Father."

Strategies for Shared Time, Toil, and Re-creation

ONE SCENE in Disney's movie, "The Jungle Book," zooms in on a couple of birds sitting on a gnarled tree limb. The dialogue starts with one vulture asking, "What do you want to do?" The other feathered creature shrugs and responds with, "I don't know. What do you want to do?" Then the first bird sighs and continues, "I don't know. What do you want to do?"

Sometimes when we step aside from our day-to-day responsibilities, we can find ourselves unsure of our own needs and locked into taking each other's recreational and social temperature. On the other hand, we may have very definite desires and plans as individuals; so that things like football games, cleaning the garage, or eating at a restaurant together become items to *negotiate* with a spouse. It's important to take responsibility for personal needs, and needs we have as couples, so that successful negotiations can take place.

A Balanced Life of Shared Intimacies

We have already established the need to spend time cultivating an abiding friendship and communicating with one another about our lives. Beyond and behind the question of spending time together are choices about what to do with the time we have. Choosing a spouse as my first "interest" or "activity" in life means making room for a spouse's ever-changing and developing desires and activities.

Let's look at the recreational intimacy that involves leisure activities, forms of adult "play," that can protect us from being too serious or one-sided as a couple. We can be re-created together by activities like jogging that restore us physically, or by taking a course together to experience intellectual sharing, or by socializing with friends. The goal is not so much to be entertained as to participate in something that rejuvenates, and complements the kinds of work we both do on a day-to-day basis.

Recreational intimacy presupposes two people with a healthy sense of self, who are willing to bring talents, interests, occupations, and needs together. When this is true, then what is happening in spiritual, recreational, and occupational arenas of each person's life can become a starting point. Recreation can also include activities that complement other areas of life. For example, sharing what has happened at work, or a few paragraphs in a book that one spouse is reading can provide an opportunity for new sharing. In our marriage, Therese can combine photography and drawing with John's fishing trips to a nearby lake. Paul's interest in boating can sometimes be combined with Anna's desire to entertain a few friends.

On the other hand, some couples enjoy a kind of "parallel play" that gives them space for individual needs. Not many of us expect to accompany a spouse to work each day, but when it comes to leisure time we don't have as much clarity about who is invited to what party. Some couples find it helpful to schedule time spent alone, as well as time spent together. Other couples, especially those with two extroverted partners prefer to spend a lot of their free time as a couple with other people. There are many options in terms of scheduling time together.

It's important to find a rhythm to your shared life that works for both of you. When there is an underlying balance to shared life, then spontaneous moments and decisions don't become times when whole layers of expectations explode in both partners' faces. Alice found herself cooking three hot meals a day when Ray first retired. As her agitation mounted, she realized that spending all these elaborate meal-times with Ray was too much togetherness. They talked about it and settled for just a quick lunch and a hot supper together.

Link between Intimacy and Time

The goal is building a shared life that includes the capacity to live out a variety of intimate possibilities. We can be enriched by experiences that stem from each partner's personal strengths. A spouse's interests can help us enter into a new arena of life. It's also important to realize that the richness of shared experiences is affected by our attitude toward time itself.

Much has been said about "quality time" together and it is true that our first priority is our family. No other activity or occupation should leave us so drained on a regular basis that we have nothing left to give to our family. Spouses can act like sentinels so that there is time for many types of intimacy and activities. For example, most married couples with young children need real breaks from parenting, time for both solitude, and for "dates" together. Professional people need realistic standards about the number of hours in a work week. People who are serious about cultivating a relationship with God need a regular daily prayer time.

Family schedules and personal calendars can be overwhelming for some of us, but are also helpful tools. We use them to structure our work week and family time. We go over our schedules once a week, dividing each week into twenty-one parts (with three in each day). A large "US" or an "ALONE" with a circle around it is placed in blocks of time that we have chosen for recreation. Some couples review their family calendar once a month. White-out and erasers are an essential ingredient no matter how often you negotiate "quality time" together.

As important as spending "quality time" is, we have discovered that a Christian marriage includes something even more satisfying. Just "spending" time is too much like consuming money or things. Time is not so much a thing to gobble or squander, as a precious beat in life's pulse, a slice of the "fullness of time." Scripture reminds us: "When the fullness of time had come, God sent his Son" (Gal 4:4) so that "in [Jesus] is the fullness of Life, and in him you too find your own fulfillment" (Col 2:9). Entering into the fullness of God's time is like stepping out of clock time and into a place of timelessness. Slowing down to pray before we eat is an example of entering into the fullness of time. Taking off our watches at the beginning of an evening together is another example.

Shared Work in Marriage

Let's also consider the intimacy that can come through a shared task, or the challenge of sharing some of the roles and responsibilities of men and women. When we were first married Therese expected John to do all the handyman jobs, like cleaning the yard and disposing of our first Christmas tree. John expected Therese to keep the porches clean, since they were part of the house. After several months of moving a brittle tree from one person's domain to the other, we had a serious fight. John's solution was to take the tree into the shed one night in May, saw it into pieces, and stuff it into trash bags. What a photo opportunity!

Sociologists name several areas of work and responsibility in marriage. The roles we assume include: bread winner, housekeeper, decision maker, parent, handyman, and kinship keeper. (Remember all those Christmas

cards?) Who does what in your marriage? How does each
of you feel about the roles you assume? Which responsibilities do you share? Which of these are opportunities
for supportive intimacy as you experience them together?
Which of these areas are a source of conflict? Again, our
goal with all of these responsibilities is a shared life mea-
sured against the fullness of time that we have received
from God as gift.

One of the challenges of our present day is that "win-
ning bread" has often become a task that involves both
people in a marriage. This means that many couples find
themselves in quicksand as all the other roles shift along-
side changes in this one area. The demands of keeping
house have also changed with microwave ovens, washing
machines, and endless car trips to several different stores
for basic household goods. How these two primary roles
are handled by many couples often defies the logic of a
written job description.

Our Christian faith can act as a beacon in the midst of
these changes. The sacrament of marriage is not primarily
a contract describing jobs and benefits, devised with nit-
picking attention to rights. The sacrament of marriage is
meant to be an experience of covenant. We have vowed a
love that will be constant but ever changing in its expression. More than this, we have a God who will help us;
and is a source of wisdom, patience, and compassion that
is beyond our own inner resources.

Paul's letter to the Ephesians (5:21–33) stresses a love
for one another that is respectful, considering what our

spouse is and does as a part of our own self definition. We need humility, especially in delegating responsibilities to a spouse, who might approach a task the "wrong" way. God will help us defer to one another out of a reverence that is anchored in Jesus Christ among us.

We can have confidence in a common vision. Chances are that both spouses want a comfortable home, financial security, and stable, fruitful relationships with children, relatives and friends. So we can look at each area of life together, even though the issues underneath will change as we move through the stages in marriage. Things like recreation, sexuality, and spirituality will be renegotiated and take on different meaning in time. But our goal is always mutual interdependence and a deference to each other's gifts as we grow in a common life.

Suggestions for Sharing and Prayer

1. The types of intimacy in marriage are: spiritual, relational, sexual, recreational, and shared work. Share an example of one type that you are very satisfied with. Share what you might do to give more attention to a type of intimacy that is lacking.

2. How do feel about the idea of scheduling together? How does your spouse's work schedule affect you? How do you decide when to "date" each other? Is there something about the way personal or family schedules are decided and communicated that could be improved?

3. There are several roles in a marriage: bread winner, housekeeper, parent, decision maker, handyman, and kinship keeper. Who does what in your family? Which role do you like best? How do you support one another in these tasks? Choose *one shared* area of responsibility and list what each person does. How do you feel about this area?

4. Read Ecclesiastes 3:1–11 together prayerfully. Of the times and seasons mentioned which are most real for you as a couple right now? What does this passage say to you about time? How do you feel about the way you "spend" time together?

~ 4 ~

Enhancing Sexual Intimacy

S OME COUPLES look through stores for items like lingerie, oils, candles or other devices that might enhance their sexual relationship. We found something that helps us, a pair of masks — not the cowboy kind, or the Mardi Gras kind — but the airplane kind that keep out light. Whether or not you have searched through stores for bedroom items, it's very likely that you have thought about what could enhance your sexual relationship. We have, and the masks are a recent find.

One of the struggles in our relationship is that we have different patterns for sleeping. Therese likes to go to sleep early in a darkened bedroom and wake up early to read in bed. John prefers to read in bed late at night, and sleep late in a darkened, quiet bedroom. We spent years fighting about the light on our headboard. A pair of masks solves our sleeping problem and also provides more peace in our sexual relationship.

Sexuality is connected to every other part of our relationship. Each of us is born as man or woman. Our sexuality colors what we say and do during the day, not just how we act in the bedroom. Part of the challenge of marriage is living an integrated life as sexual beings. Most of us already know this. What is hard to know is a suc-

cessful way to let everything that affects our sexuality be
a positive influence in our erotic experiences together. The
demands of job and family life can make us more or less
capable of sexual intimacy.

Take a Look at Erotic Love

Our lives as human persons are colored by our sexuality.
Our identities as persons becomes enmeshed in our ideas
about sexuality. In reverse, the way we look at one area
like sex is also shaped by how we look at life itself. As men
and women we assign meaning to sex within the context
of life's personal meaning. Enhancing our sexual relationship often requires figuring out how life and love and sex
are connected.

The many-faceted meanings of the word "love" give us
a clue to the breadth of the dilemma. In other languages,
like New Testament Greek, there are several words for
love instead of one: *eros* — sexual attraction and love,
philos — brotherly love, *philanthropia* — humanitarian
love, and *agape* — communal, self-giving love. Erotic love
is just one kind of human experience, and needs a context. For the early Church that context was the self-giving
love of the Risen Jesus lived out in the Body of Christ.
What is the context and the vision of the human person
that provides a foundation for your views on sex?

Jesus exhibited a profound compassion for every de-
tail of the lives of his followers. The groom and the bride
at Cana would have experienced disgrace within their

close-knit community when they couldn't provide wine. Jesus discretely resolved the problem and left their newly formed dignity as a couple intact. Scripture also recounts the healing of Peter's mother-in-law. Think of the strength this healing brought to Peter and his wife as they struggled with the risks of following Jesus. Then there was Mary Magdalen who was healed emotionally, spiritually and sexually, enabling her to walk away from a life of prostitution.

The same Jesus who touched these people comes to restore us, so that we can have healthy and holy marriages. Whatever incapacitates us as sexual beings can be healed by God's love; whether it involves being healed as a victim of abuse, the rebuilding of inadequate models of affection, recovering from the trauma of abortion, letting go of sexual obsessions and sin, or turning away from the emptiness and loneliness of sex without real love.

If you need this kind of healing, take a few moments to talk to God. One man named Paul could not look at himself in the mirror, or believe that his wife found him attractive. He remembered feeling physically and sexually inadequate way back in the junior high locker room. As he asked for God's help, he pictured himself in the communal shower with warm water washing over him along with the other boy's taunts. Then he felt a strange inner heat. He saw himself grow taller and bigger, like the Incredible Hulk. A voice said, "I have given you the largeness of my Love. Be strong, my son." After that Paul noticed he had been healed of feelings of inadequacy.

Paul's story reminds us that God sees the possibility of a wholeness that includes our sexuality.

A Vision of Sexual Intimacy

Erotic love can be described in a lot of ways. Even Scripture includes a vivid portrayal of erotic love between spouses in the Song of Songs. "More delightful is your love than wine" (1:2). There is no end to humanity's fascination with the details, and nuances involved in lovemaking. Even so, it is difficult to convey all the intimacy and personal satisfaction that can be involved. We like an image from the *Foundations* newsletter by Steve and Kathy Beirne mentioned in the bibliography. They compare the sexual relationship in marriage to a kaleidoscope. While sex always involves the same two people,

> (there can be) the total absorption of passion, or at another turn, tired love amid the demands of work. Turn it again...and you see the comfort given in times of trouble or loss. Every turn reveals another way that the sexual side of marriage can uncover ever deepening love for the couple who allows true intimacy to grow between them.

The bits of colored chips in a kaleidoscope can represent bits and pieces of ourselves that come alive in a new way as we surrender our bodies to one another through lovemaking. But what are all these pieces?

What do we bring? What do we want from each other physically? What do we give? What does a husband or wife say in the giving? Such questions can be asked of the sexual relationship as a whole, or of any one encounter.

There is a particular kind of revelation of persons, helping us connect the different parts of our bodies, lives and inner selves. Sometimes conversations about sex help clarify the subjective levels of intimacy and personal satisfaction involved. Ask each other often what you would like. Discussions about time, place, and position help a couple meet each other's needs. Making sounds as you enjoy one another can add a new dimension.

Communicate about what you hope to "hear" during acts of affection, foreplay, spousal union, and the quiet afterwards. Some hope to hear their names whispered in a way that recreates. Some watch for a celebration. Some hope for glorious and abiding statements of love. If this is going to happen, then there are choices, to make, choices beyond just "Yes" or "No."

We are not saying that every intimacy between two married people should be recorded by a Hollywood producer. We are saying there will be a kind of echo in the room, a statement made by each person to the other. What do you hear? What do you feel? Sexual intimacy exists on a continuum. On one end of this imaginary line is the self-absorbed use of sex without regard for the other. "I want" is all that is heard. In the middle is a neutral activity that doesn't say much one way or the other. On the other end of the line is the mutual expression of love which can even become an explicit sign of God's love for a spouse.

A recent papal document says, that the "Total physical self giving of sexual intercourse is meant to be (both) sign and fruit of total personal self giving." When we can act out both passion and genuine concern through sex, then we are also involved in a sacramental reality. Two people become ministers of one another's love and God's love. Each becomes gift and sign of the sacrament.

Sexual intercourse is meant to be a sustaining renewal of a couple's marriage covenant. We can make whole and holy this person we have chosen, even though we continue to experience limitations and sin. This view of sexual love leads us to some guidelines based on the good news of a potentially electrifying act of blessing.

Guidelines for Sexual Love

1. My spouse's needs are a basis for expressing myself sexually, especially the need for faithfulness. There can be adventure in uncovering needs together, as we enter each other's sexual comfort zone. Telling each other what we like and what is happening becomes very important. We take an annual weekend away in a hotel where the only item on our agenda is this kind of exploration.

2. Our definition of romance is based on the goal of using sexual activity as an avenue for reverence, even

though that reverence is both assertive and passive. There is a holiness and a new wholeness that comes from touch. Experiment with the kinds of touch that both of you can enjoy, like back rubs or holding one another. Sexual enjoyment is also more attainable when there is an ongoing context of physical affection in daily life between all family members, but especially between spouses.

3. We are sexual partners and avoid using sex as a weapon of control over each other. There is an unfolding give and take between us. Our conviction is founded in the respect for the miracle of God's creation in making us men and women, and the blessing of our complementary sexuality.

Therese was changing a diaper in front of a visitor once, and referred to the little child's genitals as "the equipment of the saints." Betty was outraged at the idea that God might have anything to do with sexuality. Are you?

4. We work at a delicious and delicate balance between power and vulnerability. Each of us is willing to admit our limits as lovers and human persons, but we remain confident in God's abiding and expressive Spirit between us. We are open to the ultimate sexual vulnerability and power of conceiving a child. We are willing to explore the ways as Paul VI wrote, that "the unitive and procreative aspects of marriage are inescapably bound together." (See the Balsam book for family planning guidelines.)

Choosing God's Presence

A study by Andrew Greeley outlined in *Faithful Attraction* (New York: Tor Books, 1991) says that people who have warm images of God and who pray together are more likely to report sexually satisfying marriages. "The impact of religion, both on sexual satisfaction directly and indirectly through its interaction with sexual stimuli, is consistently important."

Still, not too many couples are interested in "the impact of religion" when they approach an intimate encounter. The impact of place is more important, with a leisurely, private spot as most desirable. What Greeley's study implies is that God can be welcomed in our bedrooms. God's presence can be that leisurely, intimate haven. We can choose God as THE PLACE. Psalm 125 describes God's dwelling as an unshakeable place "encircled by mountains, as Yahweh encircles his people now and always." Instead of concentrating on the room through breaches in sexual etiquette like, "Is that a crack in the ceiling?" or "I just washed these sheets!" maybe we can try prayer.

God can hold us, in much the same way that we hold and surround each other. We are two made into one flesh and we can be lifted into the love of God who is Trinity. God's nature is a statement about the nature of love. God is three persons in one being.

Intercourse, when it is an enactment of...a loving way of life, not only resembles the divine intimacy, but effectively causes us to be drawn into it. We become God's intimates by the sacramental power of our own intimacy. (*Embodied in Love*, Gallagher, p. 34)

Our Creator-Father can be thanked aloud for my spouse's body at the beginning of an intimate encounter or after climax. Jesus can offer an inner strength and forgiveness that helps us take off the masks we sometimes hide behind in bed. If there are actions and attitudes that cripple us and our marriages, Jesus can restore us. The Spirit can empower us to minister healing and consolation to a weary partner.

Suggestions for Sharing and Prayer

1. Draw pictures of the male and female anatomy. Label each part with the word that you are most comfortable with. In parentheses add the word you are least comfortable with. List one or two words for sexual intercourse that you prefer in conversation with your spouse. Discuss what both people have drawn and written.

2. What do you think God has to do with sexuality? If you had a "spirituality" of marriage and sacramental sexual union what would it be? How have your ideas of sexual morality affected your marriage?

3. What are your favorite places and times for sexual intimacy? What objects have enhanced your experiences?

How have your ideas about erotic intimacy changed throughout your marriage? What do you need from within yourself and from your partner to experience sexual fulfillment?

4. The Song of Songs is a passionate allegory of God's love and fidelity that uses comparisons like "Your lips are like a scarlet thread" (4:3). Read it together and thank God aloud for each part of your spouse's body.

Surviving Together Despite Hard Times

O VER THE YEARS we have had several family members with serious allergic conditions. Once our oldest daughter Rachel came close to dying of an allergic reaction to a medication. During one year's time our son Tim missed twenty-two days of school. At another point when four of us required weekly allergy treatments, John's employer switched insurance companies, and we were denied coverage for several months.

Such medical needs put a strain on us, and sometimes tax our marriage. Serious questions have to be answered. Who stays home with a sick child? Who negotiates with a doctor or an insurance company for needed care? What effect do special cleaning supplies, or diet items have on our budget? What feelings do frequent illness or lack of stamina cause in our sexual relationship, or in planning family vacations?

You have faced problems and hard times of your own that cause lots of serious questions and affect your marriage. Some areas of concern are alcohol abuse, career changes, parenting crises, unemployment, in-laws and aging parents, an untimely death in the family, and even unresolved childhood needs that cry out for attention at odd moments in our adult lives.

Who's Trying to Get Who to Do What?

Many things happen when we face serious problems together. Problems challenge the goals and plans we have as individuals and as a couple. Problems magnify personal needs, and often cause emotional reactions that are like forest fires started by a single match. Problems put a strain on the relationships between the people who are involved in facing them. Often problems cause conflict as each spouse struggles for answers and support. All these things have happened to us as we have struggled with our medical needs.

When these phenomenon occur, we need listening skills and decision making abilities, but we also need God. St. Paul wrote many epistles to communities that were in danger of being ripped apart by one problem or another. He describes what God's Spirit will do for us and between us during a crisis.

> By the mercies of God, present your bodies as a living sacrifice.... Be transformed by the renewing of your minds, so that you may discern what is the will of God. (Rm 12:1–2, NRSV)

> Live with all humility and gentleness, bearing with one another through love, striving to preserve the unity of the Spirit. (Eph 4:2–3)

Take strength from the grace which is in Christ Jesus. (2 Tim 2:1, NJB)

It takes a lot of strength to face difficulties together, a lot of thinking, a lot of selflessness. One of the first steps in receiving these gifts together is taking a deep breath and identifying the problem or monster that we face, no matter how many heads it has. This is something we can do together. We can rely on the mercy of God to help us name the situation. We can share the burden.

For example, a couple might be facing a sudden financial crisis or ongoing spending that exceeds income. The situation can be stated objectively. Contributing problems can be listed, like an unexpected bill, a difference in spending styles between spouses, underemployment, or lack of agreement about a budget. We must ask, "Who is trying to get who to do what?" Is what we expect from one another in this situation realistic? Later on we can ask ourselves what is most needed, and generate solutions.

If there are many problems stacked on top of each other, what problem do we address first? Can we prioritize questions to be tackled? How can each of us accept responsibility for this mess? Accusing our spouse of *being* the problem, or the devil incarnate who has ruined everything, won't solve anything. Neither will expecting a spouse to fix things immediately, as if he or she were God.

Feelings, Feelings, and More Than Feelings

Problems generate lots of questions. Each question is usually accompanied by a small station wagon full of feelings. It becomes more difficult to drive toward a destination and a solution, without taking the weight of all the feelings into account. So another beginning point is to pull the car over to the side of the road, lay aside decisions, and talk about how we feel about the situation. Remember, it is very important to use "I" statements when describing feelings and to listen for our spouse's feelings as well.

Feelings remind us that something needs to be done and quicker than soon! Things are bubbling and moving and even bunching up inside and between us. Feelings are immediate and often very personal, but they are a neutral reality until we decide what to do with them. Anger, joy, fear, sadness, and compassion are parts of the human person. We see all of these in the gospel portraits of Jesus. We also see that his surrender to the Father included all these emotions. We too can name our feelings in God's presence, and to our spouse as a way of growing in relational intimacy.

Each married couple has already adopted a unique pattern for sharing and dealing with feelings. It's good to be aware of what that pattern looks like. Do we allow the expression of a wide range of feelings? Do we classify some feelings as good and others as bad? Do we let each other be responsible for our own feelings, or do we rush in and take over a spouse's emotional life? Do we support one another in efforts to deal with difficult feelings?

Which Way Are We Headed?

Once we recognize a problem and our emotional responses to it, then we are actually in a position to do something. We can generate ideas and new ways of behaving without tripping all over each other. To return to the financial example, a couple might entertain the idea of sending one spouse on a job hunt, renegotiate the family budget, take out a loan, or get help with depression-induced spending. The solutions that are chosen will have a great deal to do with our financial goals, the over-all goals of the marriage, and our shared Christian beliefs.

Solutions to problems can become new goals, and also challenge other existing short term goals, as well as the long term goals that we share. These new goals and priorities will affect daily life in a very pronounced way. Many couples experience this kind of challenge when they face a pregnancy, for example. What will happen to us? What does all this mean? What do we want most in the long run? It's important to take a serious look at our goals from time to time. A crisis can provide such an opportunity, even if it is an unwelcome and uncomfortable introduction to this task in our relationship.

Two Porcupines in Love

It's much more pleasant to consider other kinds of intimacy that aren't so much work or so much wear and tear on the nerves. Facing hard times together can feel like a mating ritual between two porcupines. Ouch! For most of us facing problems means conflict, since we are both going to see the problem from our own threatened point of view. Often we are both going to have sharp edges and defensive postures. We like the description in James:

> You want something and you lack it; so you kill. You have an ambition that you cannot satisfy; so you fight to get your way by force. (Jas 4:2–3, NJB)

It would be foolish not to expect real differences and needs to emerge. James urges us to turn to God for what we need, with a heart that is mindful of the needs of others. It sounds like a contradiction but there can be prayerful conflict between us, if we view each other as brother and sister in Christ instead of enemies. Then we can acknowledge pain, limitations, irresponsible behavior, and sin between us. We can see ourselves as being on the same side in a fight, or at least willing to be reconciled. We can let go of our position and be reshaped, transformed, converted together in God's sight.

Seek Healing and Support

When a serious problem emerges we can be tempted to open an imaginary tool box to ease the conflict between us. One spouse might use a saw to sever the relationship for a time. Another might choose a hammer to drive a point of view; another, a screwdriver to nag and tighten the pressure; still another, a pair of pliers to appease and cling on for dear life. Searching for an answer and a tool is a good thing, but what kind of a tool?

Using many resources is a key to a healthier marriage, as seen in the statement made by Joseph and Lois Bird in the classic book *Marriage is For Grownups* (Garden City, New York: Doubleday, 1971).

> Most problems...are seldom, if ever, singular, identifiable, problems, per se, but are, rather, learned patterns of behavior, usually on the part of both spouses, which involve the total relation-ship...faulty perceptions, irrational thinking, and irresponsible behavior.

Our first tool is a willingness to face ourselves, within the context of a daily relationship with God. Jesus knows us better than we do ourselves, and will help us face our own behavior and needs. As we pray and study our faith in a regular way, we can regain a vision of the basic good-ness of self and spouse. We can ask God's help and expect new insights. Jesus empowers us to be instruments of each other's salvation and wholeness.

Another source of support is the primary community that we are a part of as a married couple, whether that be with relatives, friends, or the local church. We need a place where we can tell our story, without hearing excessive amounts of advice or criticism. If we have no such community, or belong to a fragmented and unsupportive group, then it may be time to find one. Many parishes offer small faith sharing groups, or Bible study groups. Connections with such a community can relieve a lot of pressure.

Finally, consider all the resources of the larger Christian community such as Marriage Encounter weekends, courses on family life, healing Masses, the Retrouvaille program for troubled marriages, or professional counseling. We have also experienced support and healing for our marriage through other sacraments, especially the sacrament of reconciliation. We once celebrated this sacrament with a priest friend and just the two of us. It was a special chance to look at the failings in our relationship, as well as our individual sins. Therese actually experienced physical healing as a kind of "side effect" of the sacrament.

Suggestions for Sharing and Prayer

1. Explore the role that feelings play in your relationship. Which emotions are most often expressed between you — anger, joy, fear, sadness, loneliness, or compassion? Which emotions are the most uncomfortable for you to share? What is it like for you to acknowledge your spouse's emotions?

2. Write and share "feelings" prayers:

Lord, I feel like a (name an animal).
Help me when I feel like (describe the animal's action).
And God says, _____

Pray aloud together, telling God how you feel about the most pressing needs in your lives. Search out a Psalm that names similar feelings. Read it aloud together.

3. When you experience conflict and open an imaginary tool box to ease the pain, do you grab a saw to sever the relationship, a hammer to drive home your point, a nagging screwdriver, or a pair of appeasing pliers? Why?

4. Make a list of personal long range goals. Make a list of what you think are the long range goals you have as a couple. Compare lists. How has your behavior as an individual brought you closer to or further from realizing the goals you have as a couple?

~ 6 ~

Blessing Children, Family and Strangers

===============

L AST YEAR we had a family religious education session on Baptism with our junior high son and our preschool daughter. We assembled a large glass bowl, a little holy water, and a newborn doll named Brian. As we practiced tracing the sign of the cross on Brian, John pretended to sneeze several times. Each time someone responded with, "God bless you!" Of course, this was planned to help us discuss what it means to bless each other, and to belong to Jesus as a family.

Marriage itself, by its very nature is meant to be a source of life and blessing. The sacramental partnership between female and male is God's creation. The universal *Catechism of the Catholic Church* (Ligouri Pub., 1994) describes the importance of marriage in God's plan for giving human and divine life to the world.

> Their mutual love becomes an image of the absolute and unfailing love with which God loves.... This love which God blesses is intended to be fruitful and to be realized in the common work of watching over creation.

In a sense, the same Spirit that hovered over the waters at the germination of the universe calls us together as a source of blessing for everything around us. Rosa's parents in Puerto Rico took this mission of blessing very literally. The first thing each child did in the morning was to ask for a parent's blessing. In our own French Canadian heritage the father of an extended family blesses each person at a gathering on New Year's Day. Tracing the sign of the cross on each other's foreheads at bedtime is a way of recalling our baptismal life. Also blessings at meals, or when some one sneezes are small hints of the call to sanctify all we touch and do.

Consecrated for Ministry

These acts of blessing will feel hollow, unless a marriage is spiritually and emotionally healthy. No relationship turned in on itself, or warped by failings, will thrive or have the strength to serve and bless others. We must yield to the Holy Spirit at work in this sacrament who will consecrate, make holy, and empower us to give ourselves away together. For most couples this means welcoming and raising children who become life-long evidence of an ever growing bodily, emotional, financial, and spiritual love between husband and wife. Two o'clock feedings and negotiations about who drives Dad's car can stretch us and help us grow.

Whether we have children or not, the abiding intimacy and friendship that we share is meant to be penetrated by the fire and breath of God's Spirit. Each marriage is a vocation to ministry of some sort. One example is found in the Acts of the Apostles. Aquila and Priscilla were tent makers whose Corinthian home was the center of an early Christian community. They also moved to Ephesus with Paul and established a new home that became an adult catechetical center for that community.

It's good to ask what ministry flows out of your marriage. Is your primary concern raising Christian children, or providing care for members of your extended families, or serving strangers, or even a ministry to social institutions or the environment? Do you see your job as an opportunity for ministry? What do you spend yourselves on together? In our marriage we have been fortunate enough to combine a ministry to five children with work as religious educators in the Church. Ed and Irene, friends of ours with adult children, have experienced a call to serve elderly neighbors. Roy and Denise adopted two abused children.

Domestic Sanctuary

The base of operation for any kind of ministry is the home. Stepping across the threshold is meant to be like entering a prophetic re-enactment of God's kingdom among us, not like a spiritual Disneyland, but a workshop on love. Our first task is to create a real place where anyone can see, hear, and touch Jesus alive among us. A palace dedicated to individualism with televisions in every room, or a boarding house where people make pit stops between appointments won't do. We face the challenge of building households where prayer and honest conversations are the norm of daily life.

We need households of faith where we can "encourage one another and build one another up" (1 Thes 5:11). We are called to build sanctuaries, to "love one another with mutual affection; anticipate one another in showing honor" (Rm 12:10). This is the basis for the Church's insistence that parents are the primary religious educators of their own children. We teach by what we try to live.

For almost ten years this desire to be both a domestic sanctuary, and a household of faith has also led us to include a single friend named Dan in our family. The three adults in our home share morning prayer together four days a week. We guard each other's personal needs as well, and share some resources like Dan's tent, for camping trips.

The church is meant to be a vital network of households and families, a community of real places of faith with different gifts that become interdependent. Families must find ways to support each other — child care, places for single people to celebrate holidays, used clothing, meals during an illness, and transportation to liturgies.

Hospitality to Brothers and Sisters

The Gospels have a strange habit of reducing all kinds of relationships to that of brothers and sisters. Opening our homes to others, and even caring for our own children means seeing them as equal in God's sight. In a sense, all those to whom we minister the love of Jesus have a right to our hospitality, our food and a listening heart, even though it means dying to self.

The Scriptures also see children as a blessing from God. In the past, this was obvious when parents needed children to help on the farm. Now it is up to us to choose children as gift for their own sake. In our family, Mary was born as a Christmas gift, and Timothy was literally an Epiphany gift from God. Have you chosen your own children, parents, or relatives as gift? Have you thanked God for each one by name? Have you recognized and adopted friends or neighbors as brothers or sisters in Jesus?

Another part of our ministry to different generations is building a well balanced life together. The society around us exerts pressures that drive families apart. Children are expected to play and go to school. Adults are expected to work. Elders are expected to enjoy a leisurely retirement. Often each of these pursuits are scheduled and organized to exclude the other generations in a family.

The truth is that each of us needs play, work, education, and rest. As married couples we can provide a model for an integrated life. As parents we can help children make choices that ensure the kind of balance that they need in order to thrive. For example, there can be limits on the amount of television or organized sports, especially for the sake of eating together. Children can have regular, assigned housekeeping jobs. Young people can be included in regular visits to elderly family members. Dinner guests can bring food items, or help with clean up.

Evangelize Each Other and the World

A document on evangelization by the National Conference of Catholic Bishops, called *Go and Make Disciples,* reminds us that our ultimate goal as believing married couples involved in service, hospitality, or acts of blessing, is evangelization:

> ...bringing the Good News of Jesus into every human situation and seeking to convert individuals and society by the divine power of the Gospel itself. It's essence is the proclamation of salvation in Jesus Christ and the response of a person in faith, both being the work of the Spirit of God.

Maybe you never thought of yourselves as evangelists. Whether you have or not, your marriage, and even your home, stands as a sign or a statement about the ultimate meaning of life. If you are brave enough, ask a few honest friends what they hear and see behind your relationship. Is it the Good News of Jesus Christ? Or do you need a new theme song?

When we marry in Christ we can give each other permission to be evangelists; not to preach at each other, but to act out of an awareness of the real mercy of a loving God toward a spouse. For a married couple the question is not, "Do I want to bring you to God?" but

"How am I bringing you closer or driving you away from God?"

With this understanding comes a new strength to reach out to others. We will be able to pray more concretely, include family members in celebrations of faith, and share the message of the Gospel as it touches our lives. Last month as Therese was working at our home computer she heard a knock on the door. She was met by a young woman whose deceased grandparents lived in our home twenty years ago. After a brief visit, Linda shared a dream about her grandmother and her fears about her own serious illness. Then she asked, "Do you believe in dreams?" It was the perfect chance to share faith and pray for God's healing.

The Journey Home to God

Ushering others into God's presence brings us that much closer to our own destiny. Marriage is a journey home together. First we build a home, a nest, a glorious place never before experienced in human history. We create a space for love to flourish. Then we welcome people into our home and give away all of our food, money, our time and ourselves. If we are lucky we lavish our energy on children, community, and even angels disguised as strangers. Then we send them all off to their own homes so we can get ready for the final journey to God.

Do you ever stop and look at the way God has shaped

your whole journey through marriage? You were called into being through the relationship between your own parents. Life itself was often the fruit of the sacrament of marriage, and the desire to nourish and sustain love. Therese wears her grandmother's wedding ring as a reminder of God's love so clearly evident in her grandparents and parents. How gracious our God and rightly to be praised!

Do you see God's gift in giving you a companion for life's adult journey? You were called, consecrated, and then became instruments of each other's eternal destiny. You have been given a friend to wait with, to accept, to endure life with, to trust. What condition is that friendship in now? What do you want of that married relationship in the future?

We hope to be faithful to choices and statements made twenty-five years ago. We placed a golden cross interlaced with two rings on our wedding cake instead of a bride and groom. God is love and we have chosen God. Also, through our marriage we hope to echo the words of thanksgiving engraved inside John's wedding ring: "Praise God!"

Suggestions for Sharing and Prayer

1. How do you feel about your ability to relate to children, elderly, and strangers? What are your spouse's strengths in this area? What challenges do you face now?

2. What are ways that you practice hospitality as a married couple and as a household? How could you grow in the area of hospitality? Who is God inviting you to reach out to — extended family, neighbors, friends?

3. What ministry or service is an outgrowth of your marriage? What needs do you have as a household that you might bring to the local Christian community?

4. How do you feel about the call to be instruments of each other's salvation? What are the ways you might "evangelize" one another, and reveal God's love?

5. The Vatican II document on the laity calls the family "the domestic sanctuary of the church." Where would you place your family on the continuum below? Why?

---

domestic sanctuary   insane asylum

Bibliography

Allen, Karen and Gary. *Roots and Wings*. Cleveland, OH: Pilgrim Press, 1992.

Balsam, Charles and Elizabeth. *Family Planning: A Guide for Exploring the Issues*. Ligouri, MO: Ligouri Pub, 1994.

Boucher, John. *Following Jesus: A Disciple's Guide to Discerning God's Will*. Pecos, NM: Dove Publications, 1995.

Boucher, John and Therese. "Marriage in the Power of the Spirit," audio tapes. CRS of LI, Box 7338, Hicksville, NY 11801.

Boucher, Therese. *Spiritual Grandparenting*. New York: Crossroad, 1991.

Catechism of the Catholic Church. Ligouri, MO: Ligouri Pub, 1994.

Conway, Jim and Sally. *Traits of a Lasting Marriage*. Downer's Grove, IL: Intervarsity Press, 1991.

Dominian, Jack. *Dynamics of Marriage*. Mystic, CT: Twenty-Third Pub, 1993.

Elliott, Peter. *What God Has Joined.... The Sacramentality of Marriage*. Staten Island, NY: Alba House Pub, 1989.

Ensley, Eddie. *Prayer that Heals Our Emotions*. Columbus, GA: Contemplative Books, 1986.

Finley, Mitch. *Your Family in Focus*. Notre Dame, IN: Ave Maria Press, 1993.

Follow the Way of Love. Washington, DC: United States Catholic Conference, Inc, 1994.

"Foundations: A Newsletter for Newly Married Couples." Box 1632. Portland, ME 04104.

Gallagher, Charles, et al. *Embodied in Love: Sacramental Spirituality and Sexual Intimacy*. New York: Crossroad, 1984.

Louden, Jennifer. *The Couples Comfort Book*. San Francisco, CA: Harper, 1994.

Other Titles Available from Resurrection Press

Discovering Your Light	*Margaret O'Brien*	$6.95
The Gift of the Dove	*Joan M. Jones, PCPA*	$3.95
Healing through the Mass	*Robert DeGrandis, SSJ*	$7.95
His Healing Touch	*Michael Buckley*	$7.95
Let's Talk	*James P. Lisante*	$7.95
A Celebration of Life	*Anthony Padovano*	$7.95
Miracle in the Marketplace	*Henry Libersat*	$5.95
Common Bushes Afire with God	*Kieran Kay, OFM*	$8.95
Heart Business	*Dolores Torrell*	$6.95
A Path to Hope	*John Dillon*	$5.95
The Healing of the Religious Life	*Faricy/Blackborow*	$6.95
Transformed by Love	*Margaret Magdalen, CSMV*	$5.95
RVC Liturgical Series: Our Liturgy		$4.25
	The Great Seasons	$3.95
	The Liturgy of the Hours	$3.95
	The Lector's Ministry	$3.95
Catholic Is Wonderful	*Mitch Finley*	$4.95
Behold the Man	*Judy Marley, SFO*	$3.50
A Rachel Rosary		$3.50
Still Riding the Wind	*George Montague, SM*	$7.95
In the Power of the Spirit	*Kevin Ranaghan*	$6.95
Lights in the Darkness	*Ave Clark, O.P.*	$8.95
Practicing the Prayer of Presence	*van Kaam/Muto*	$7.95
Stress and the Search for Happiness	*Muto/van Kaam*	$3.95
Harnessing Stress	*Muto/van Kaam*	$3.95
Healthy and Holy under Stress	*Muto/van Kaam*	$3.95

Spirit-Life Audiocassette Collection

Celebrating the Vision of Vatican II	*Michael Himes*	$6.95
Hail Virgin Mother	*Robert Lauder*	$6.95
Praying on Your Feet	*Robert Lauder*	$6.95
Annulment: Healing-Hope-New Life	*Thomas Molloy*	$6.95
Life After Divorce	*Tom Hartman*	$6.95
Divided Loyalties	*Anthony Padovano*	$6.95
Path to Hope	*John Dillon*	$6.95
Thank You Lord!	*McGuire/DeAngelis*	$8.95
Spirit Songs	*Jerry DeAngelis*	$9.95

Resurrection Press books and cassettes are available in your local religious bookstore. If you want to be on our mailing list for our up-to-date announcements, please write or phone:

Resurrection Press
P.O. Box 248, Williston Park, NY 11596
1-800-89 BOOKS